AMAZING

grace

AMAZING

grace

MESSAGES of HOPE
in SCRIPTURE
and VERSE

PLAIN SIGHT PUBLISHING
AN IMPRINT OF CEDAR FORT, INC.
SPRINGVILLE, UTAH

ANGELA D. BAXTER

ISBN 13: 978-1-4621-1501-3

Published by Plain Sight Publishing, an imprint of Cedar Fort, Inc.
2373 W. 700 S., Springville, UT 84663
Distributed by Cedar Fort, Inc., www.cedarfort.com

Cover and page design by Angela D. Baxter
Cover design © 2014 by Lyle Mortimer

Printed in China

10 9 8 7 6 5 4 3 2 1

for ROBERT

grace *n.*\grās\

1. Unmerited divine assistance given humans
   for their regeneration or sanctification.

2. A virtue coming from God.

3. A state of sanctification enjoyed
   through divine grace.

WHEN JOHN NEWTON WROTE the lines that would become the beloved hymn *Amazing Grace*, it was to accompany his sermon for New Year's Day 1773. An Anglican priest and curate of Olney, Newton often composed hymns to enhance his sermons' meaning and make them more memorable. Though many of Newton's hymns had personal connections for him, none has become as universal as *Amazing Grace*, probably the most famous of all folk hymns.

"Faith's Review and Expectation," as Newton entitled it, describes the joy and peace of a once-wretched soul, brought from despair to salvation through the mercy and grace of God. In the hymn's words, Newton was reflecting on his own life, sharing his heartfelt expression of gratitude to God for his own redemption.

In his early years, Newton was headstrong and disobedient. Several close encounters with death never led to any lasting change. After being press-ganged into service in the Royal Navy and subsequently discharged, Newton began a career in the slave trade.

In 1748, the merchant ship he was aboard encountered a severe storm while headed for England and nearly sank, prompting Newton to pray to God for mercy. That day, March 21, 1748, became one Newton remembered for the rest of his life. It was the day of his conversion and deliverance. Although he continued to work in the slave trade after his conversion, he saw to it that the slaves under his care were treated humanely. He later said that his true conversion did not happen until some time later and admitted that it was "a subject of humiliating reflection to me . . . that I was once an active instrument in a business at which my heart now shudders."

Once Newton had put his seafaring days behind him, he began to study Christian theology and was ordained in the Church of England in 1764. In his later years, he even joined in England's fight for the abolition of slavery, inspiring his friend William Wilberforce, the main champion of the cause.

Amazing Grace was first printed in 1779 in *Olney Hymns*, Newton's collaboration with poet William Cowper. In 1835, the lyrics were joined to the melody "New Britain," creating the hymn familiar today. The beloved hymn has since become an inspiring and hopeful anthem for people all over the world.

SOURCES

"Grace," Merriam-Webster.com, http://www.merriam-webster.com/dictionary/grace; accessed April 7, 2014.

"The Creation of 'Amazing Grace,'" http://www.loc.gov/item/ihas.200149085; accessed April 4, 2014.

Amazing Grace: The Story of America's Most Beloved Song (New York: Harper Perennial, 2003).

Amazing Grace in America: Our Spiritual National Anthem (Angel City Press 1996).

AMAZING
grace

*A*ND HE SAID unto me, My grace is sufficient for thee: for my strength is made perfect in weakness. Most gladly therefore will I rather glory in my infirmities, that the power of Christ may rest upon me.

2 CORINTHIANS 12:9

AND OF HIS FULNESS

have all we received, and grace for grace.

JOHN 1:16

THE *sound*

*A*ND AFTER the earthquake a fire; but the Lord was not in the fire: and after the fire a still small voice.

1 KINGS 19:12

HE IS DESPISED and rejected of men; a man of sorrows, and acquainted with grief: and we hid as it were our faces from him; he was despised, and we esteemed him not.

SURELY HE HATH borne our griefs, and carried our sorrows: yet we did esteem him stricken, smitten of God, and afflicted.

BUT HE WAS wounded for our transgressions, he was bruised for our iniquities: the chastisement of our peace was upon him; and with his stripes we are healed.

ISAIAH 53:3–5

THAT

saved

A WRETCH *like* ME

THESE THINGS I have spoken unto you, that in me ye might have peace. In the world ye shall have tribulation: but be of good cheer; I have overcome the world.

JOHN 16:33

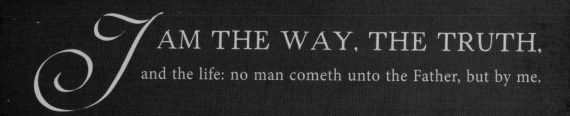

I AM THE WAY, THE TRUTH, and the life: no man cometh unto the Father, but by me.

JOHN 14:6

I once

TRUST IN THE Lord
with all thine heart; and lean not
unto thine own understanding.
IN ALL THY ways acknowledge
him, and he shall direct thy paths.

PROVERBS 3:5–6

N
OW THE GOD of hope fill you with all joy and peace in believing, that ye may abound in hope, through the power of the Holy Ghost.

ROMANS 15:13

AM

found

SK, AND IT shall be given you; seek, and ye shall find; knock, and it shall be opened unto you.

MATTHEW 7:7

FOR WHICH CAUSE we faint not; but though our outward man perish, yet the inward man is renewed day by day.

FOR OUR LIGHT affliction, which is but for a moment, worketh for us a far more exceeding and eternal weight of glory;

WHILE WE LOOK not at the things which are seen, but at the things which are not seen: for the things which are seen are temporal; but the things which are not seen are eternal.

2 CORINTHIANS 4:16–18

WAS

blind

BUT
NOW

*For now we see through a glass, darkly; but then face to face: now
I know in part; but then shall I know even as also I am known.*

1 CORINTHIANS 13:12

I see

'Twas

GRACE

For by grace

FOR BY GRACE are ye saved through faith; and that not of yourselves: it is the gift of God.

EPHESIANS 2:8

L

ET THE WORD of Christ dwell in you richly in all wisdom; teaching and admonishing one another in psalms and hymns and spiritual songs, singing with grace in your hearts to the Lord.

COLOSSIANS 3:16

THAT

Laught

*F*ROM THE END of the earth will I cry unto thee, when my heart is overwhelmed: lead me to the rock that is higher than I.

PSALM 61:2

𝓕OR GOD HATH
not given us the spirit of fear;
but of power, and of love, and of
a sound mind.

2 TIMOTHY 1:7

TO *fear*

AND *grace*

N EITHER IS THERE

salvation in any other: for there is none

other name under heaven given among

men, whereby we must be saved.

ACTS 4:12

*P*EACE I leave with you, my peace I give unto you: not as the world giveth, give I unto you. Let not your heart be troubled, neither let it be afraid.

JOHN 14:27

MY *fears* RELIEVED

HOW
precious

EVERY GOOD GIFT and
every perfect gift is from above, and cometh
down from the Father of lights, with whom is
no variableness, neither shadow of turning.

JAMES 1:17

A ND I SAY unto you,

Ask, and it shall be given you;

seek, and ye shall find;

knock, and it shall be opened unto you.

LUKE 11:9

DID THAT
GRACE
appear

THE
HOUR

Jesus said unto him, If thou canst believe, all things are possible to him that believeth.

MARK 9:23

I FIRST
believed

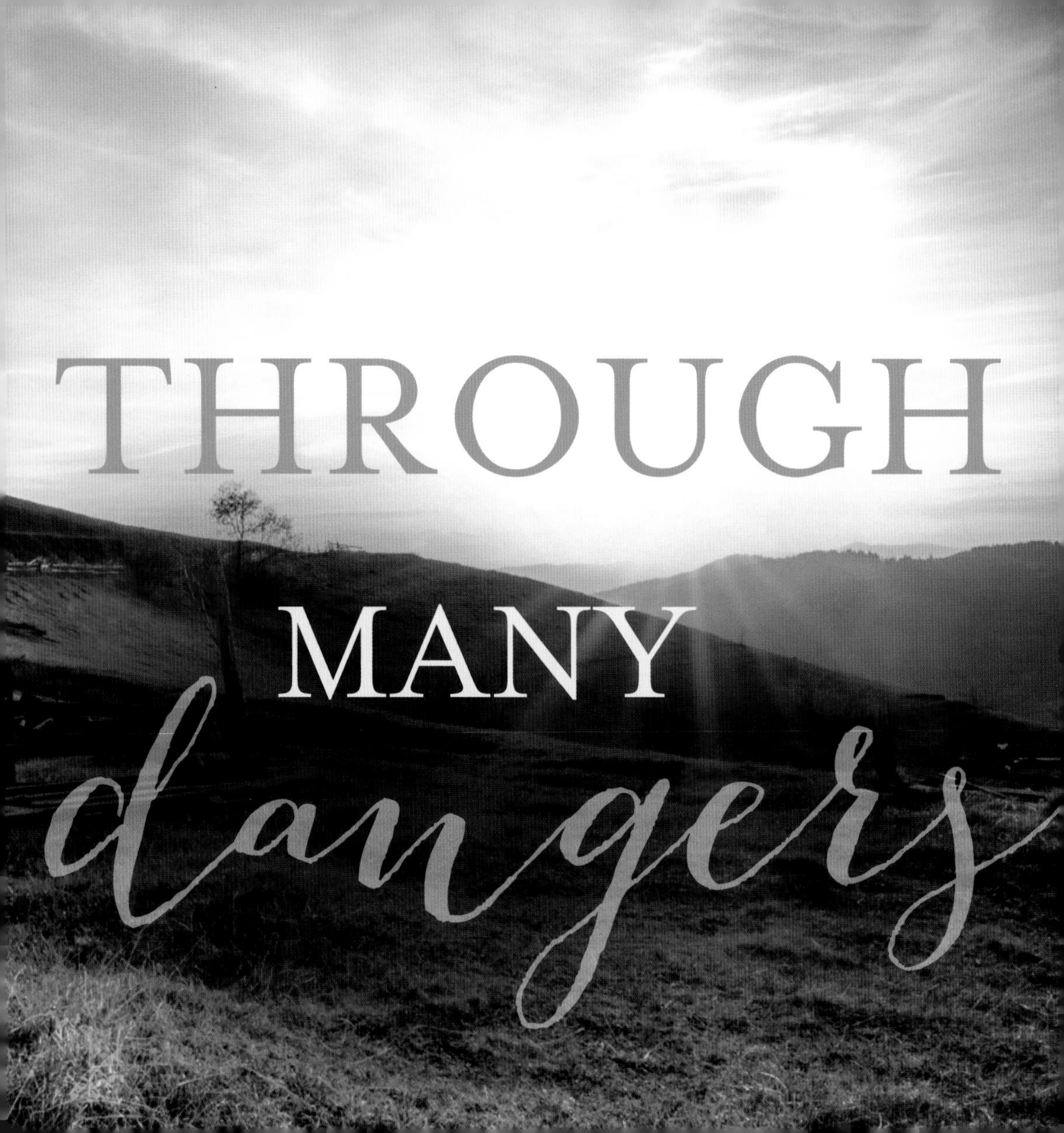
THROUGH
MANY
dangers

BUT NOW THUS saith the Lord that created thee, O Jacob, and he that formed thee, O Israel, Fear not: for I have redeemed thee, I have called thee by thy name; thou art mine.

WHEN THOU PASSEST through the waters, I will be with thee; and through the rivers, they shall not overflow thee: when thou walkest through the fire, thou shalt not be burned; neither shall the flame kindle upon thee.

FOR I AM the Lord thy God, the Holy One of Israel, thy Saviour.

ISAIAH 43:1–3

*T*HERE HATH NO temptation taken you but such as is common to man: but God is faithful, who will not suffer you to be tempted above that ye are able; but will with the temptation also make a way to escape, that ye may be able to bear it.

1 CORINTHIANS 10:13

Toils

AND

snares

I HAVE
already
COME

HAVE NOT I commanded thee? Be strong and of a good courage; be not afraid, neither be thou dismayed: for the Lord thy God is with thee whithersoever thou goest.

JOSHUA 1:9

AND HE SAID unto me, My grace is sufficient for thee: for my strength is made perfect in weakness. Most gladly therefore will I rather glory in my infirmities, that the power of Christ may rest upon me.

2 CORINTHIANS 12:9

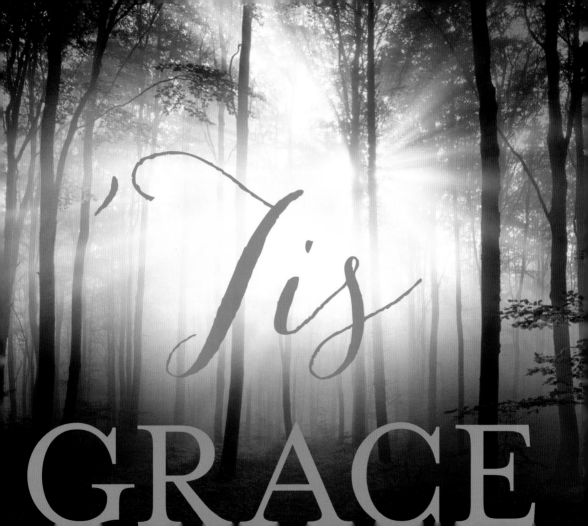

'Tis

GRACE

FEAR THOU NOT; for I am with thee: be not dismayed; for I am thy God: I will strengthen thee; yea, I will help thee; yea, I will uphold thee with the right hand of my righteousness.

ISAIAH 41:10

THE LORD IS my shepherd;
I shall not want.
HE MAKETH ME to lie
down in green pastures: he leadeth me beside the
still waters.

HE RESTORETH MY soul: he
leadeth me in the paths of righteousness for his
name's sake.

YEA, THOUGH I walk through the
valley of the shadow of death, I will fear no evil:
for thou art with me; thy rod and thy staff they
comfort me.

PSALM 23:1–4

safe

THUS

FAR

AND

grace

L

ET US THEREFORE come boldly
unto the throne of grace, that we may obtain mercy,
and find grace to help in time of need.

HEBREWS 4:16

WILL

LEAD

ME

Then spake Jesus again unto them, saying, I am the light of the world: he that followeth me shall not walk in darkness, but shall have the light of life.

JOHN 8:12

The
LORD

SEEK YE the Lord while he may be found,
call ye upon him while he is near.

ISAIAH 55:6

COME UNTO ME, all ye that labour and are heavy laden, and I will give you rest.

TAKE MY YOKE upon you, and learn of me; for I am meek and lowly in heart: and ye shall find rest unto your souls.

FOR MY YOKE is easy, and my burden is light.

MATTHEW 11:28–30

HAS

promised

good
TO ME

BUT AS IT is written, Eye hath not seen, nor ear heard, neither have entered into the heart of man, the things which God hath prepared for them that love him.

1 CORINTHIANS 2:9

$\mathcal{I}$N THE beginning was the Word, and the Word was with God, and the Word was God.

JOHN 1:1

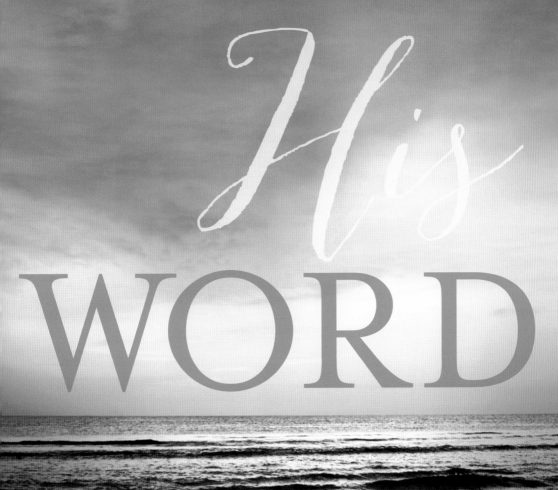

His
WORD

MY
hope
SECURES

L

OOKING UNTO JESUS
the author and finisher of our faith; who
for the joy that was set before him endured
the cross, despising the shame, and is set down at the
right hand of the throne of God.

HEBREWS 12:2

FOR I KNOW that my redeemer liveth, and that he shall stand at the latter day upon the earth.

JOB 19:25

I CAN DO all things through Christ which strengtheneth me.

PHILIPPIANS 4:13

WAIT ON THE lord: be of good

courage, and he shall strengthen thine heart.

PSALM 27:14

AND

portion

BE

AS
LONG
AS
en

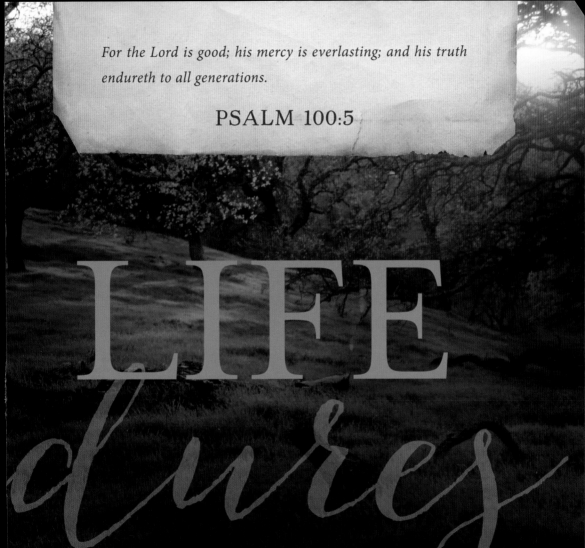

For the Lord is good; his mercy is everlasting; and his truth endureth to all generations.

PSALM 100:5

LIFE *dures*

YES, WHEN HIS *flesh*

O DEATH, WHERE is thy sting? O grave, where is thy victory? THE STING OF death is sin; and the strength of sin is the law. BUT THANKS BE to God, which giveth us the victory through our Lord Jesus Christ.

1 CORINTHIANS 15:55–57

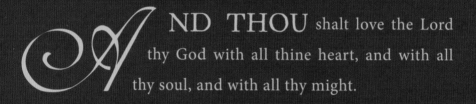

AND THOU shalt love the Lord
thy God with all thine heart, and with all
thy soul, and with all thy might.

DEUTERONOMY 6:5

AND

heart

AND GOD SHALL wipe away all tears from their eyes; and there shall be no more death, neither sorrow, nor crying, neither shall there be any more pain: for the former things are passed away.

REVELATION 21:4

*T*O EVERY THING there is
a season, and a time to every purpose under
the heaven.

ECCLESIASTES 3:1

AND
MORTAL
life

JESUS SAID UNTO her, I am the resurrection, and the life: he that believeth in me, though he were dead, yet shall he live.

AND WHOSOEVER LIVETH and believeth in me shall never die.

JOHN 11:25–26

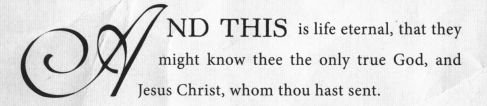

$\mathcal{A}$ND THIS is life eternal, that they might know thee the only true God, and Jesus Christ, whom thou hast sent.

JOHN 17:3

I SHALL

possess

$\mathcal{A}$ND IF I go and prepare a place for you, I will come again, and receive you unto myself; that where I am, there ye may be also.

JOHN 14:3

*A*ND JESUS said
unto them, I am the bread
of life: he that cometh to me
shall never hunger; and he that believeth on
me shall never thirst.

JOHN 6:35

A life of

OF

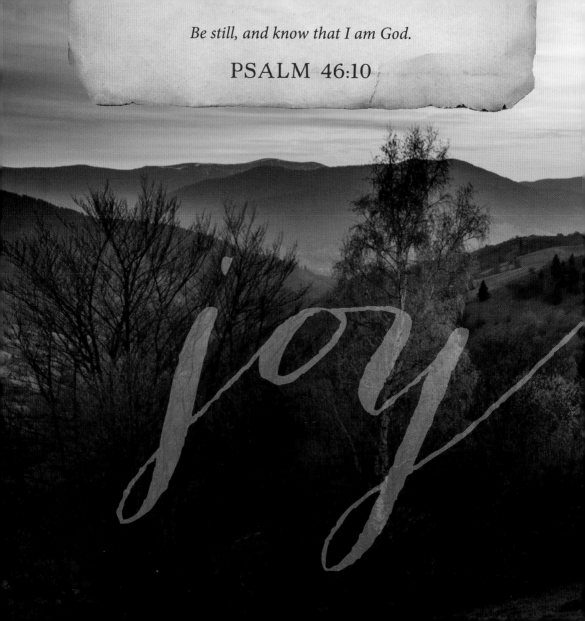

Be still, and know that I am God.

PSALM 46:10

joy

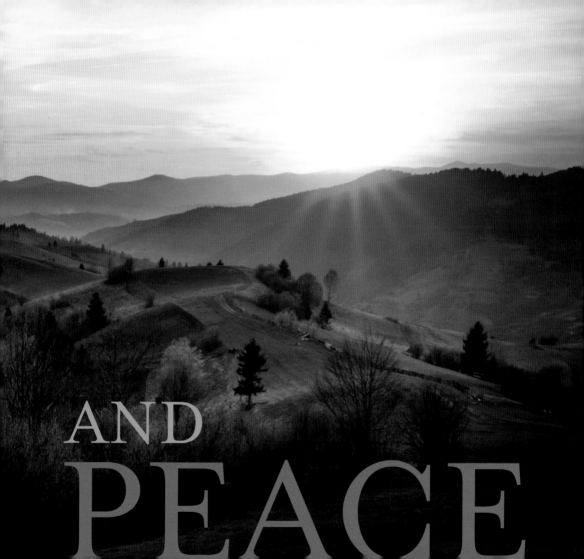

AND
PEACE

BUT NOW, O Lord, thou art our
father; we are the clay, and thou our potter;
and we all are the work of thy hand.

ISAIAH 64:8

L
O, I AM with you alway, even unto the end of the world. Amen.

MATTHEW 28:20

LIKE *snow*

C

OME NOW, AND let us reason together, saith the Lord: though your sins be as scarlet, they shall be as white as snow; though they be red like crimson, they shall be as wool.

ISAIAH 1:18

FOR THE LORD God is a sun and shield: the Lord will give grace and glory: no good thing will he withhold from them that walk uprightly.

PSALM 84:11

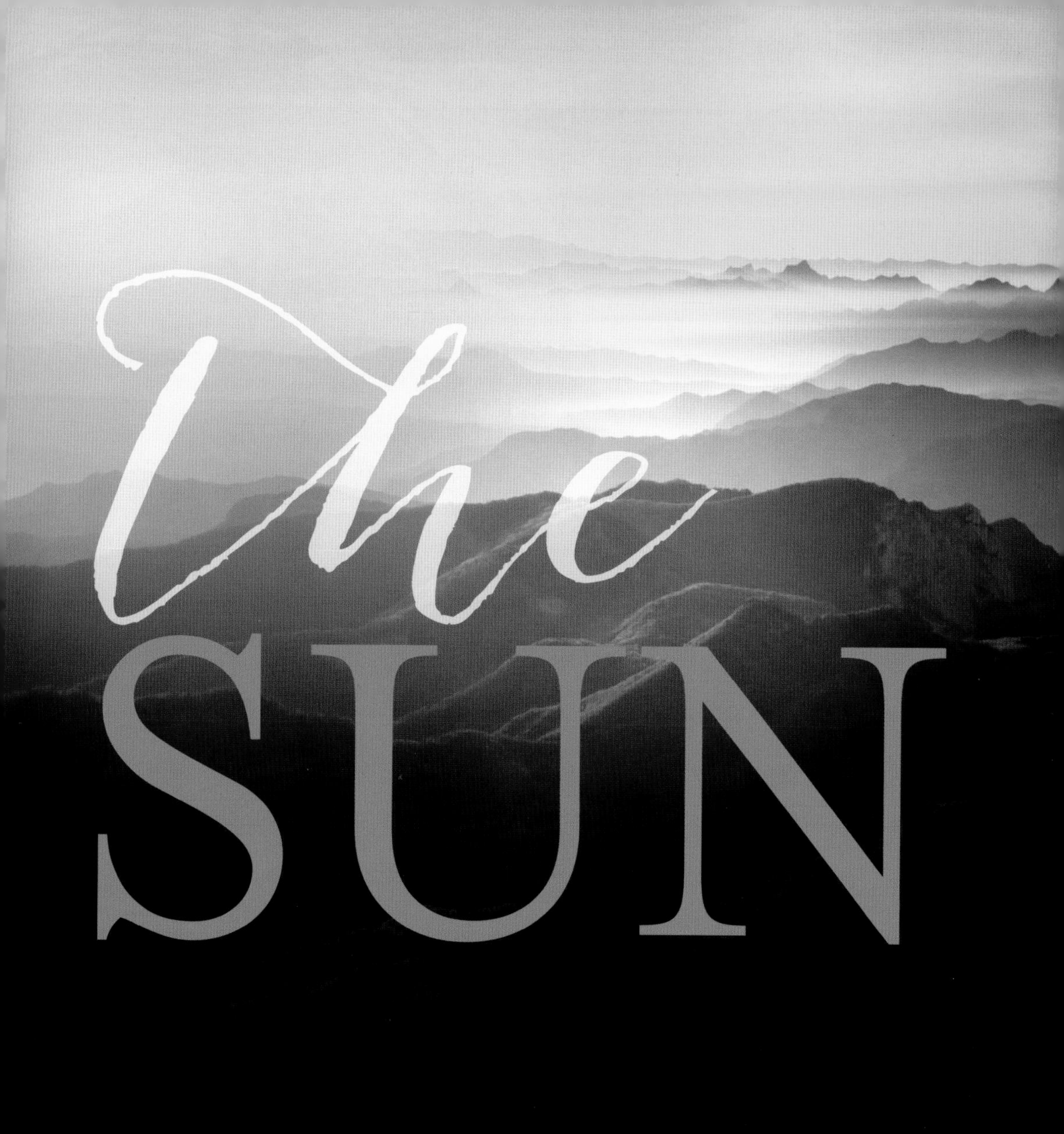

The SUN

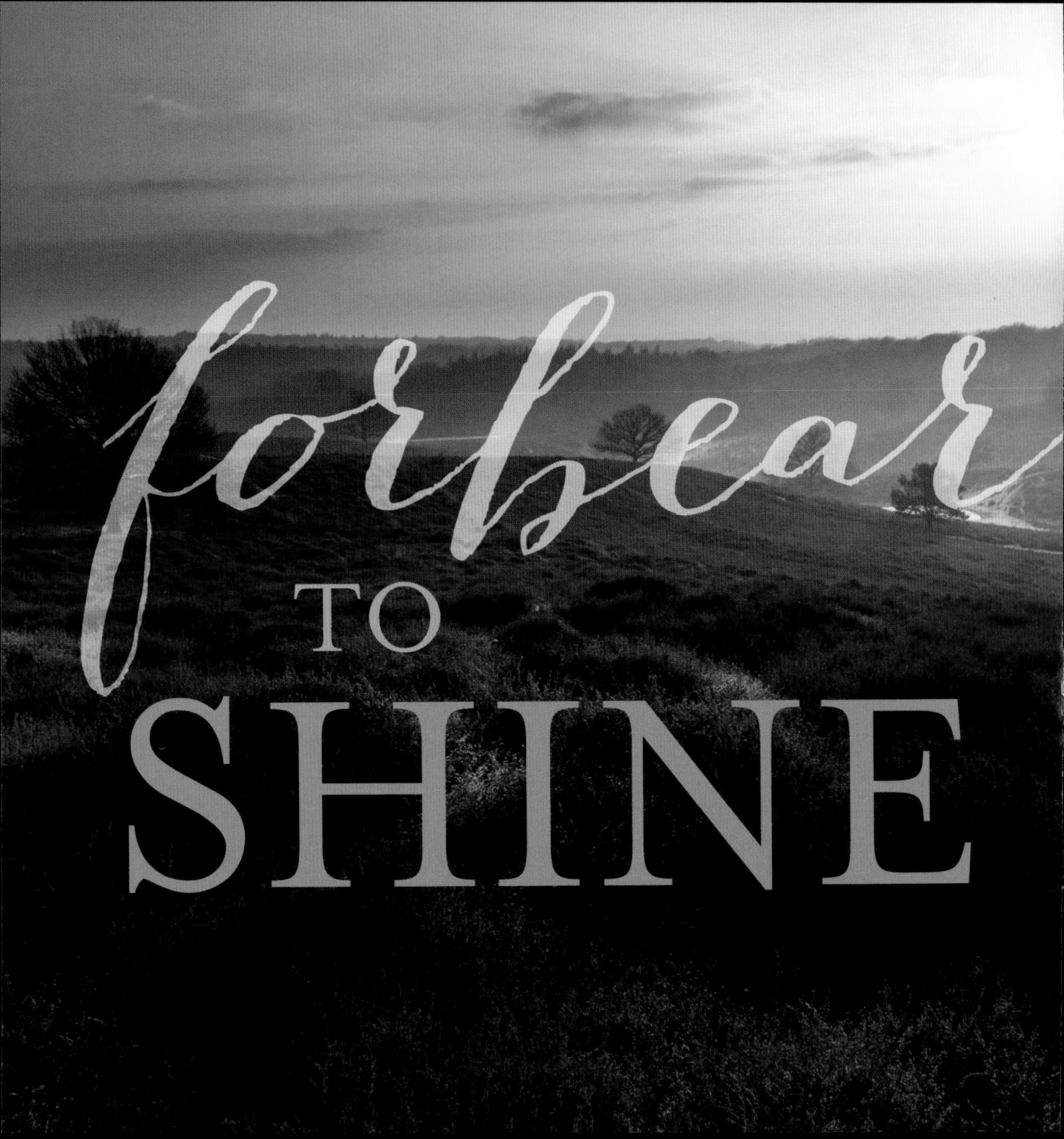

forbear

TO

SHINE

Ye are the light of the world. A city that is set on an hill cannot be hid.

NEITHER DO MEN light a candle, and put it under a bushel, but on a candlestick; and it giveth light unto all that are in the house.

LET YOUR LIGHT so shine before men, that they may see your good works, and glorify your Father which is in heaven.

MATTHEW 5:14–16

FOR GOD SO loved the world,
that he gave his only begotten Son, that whosoever believeth in him should not perish, but have everlasting life. For God sent not his Son into the world to condemn the world; but that the world through him might be saved.

JOHN 3:16–17

WHO

called

ME

*A*ND WE know that all things work together for good to them that love God, to them who are the called according to his purpose.

ROMANS 8:28

THE LORD BLESS thee, and keep thee: THE LORD MAKE his face shine upon thee, and be gracious unto thee: THE LORD LIFT up his countenance upon thee, and give thee peace.

NUMBERS 6:24–26

HERE

below

For I am persuaded, that neither death, nor life, nor angels, nor principalities, nor powers, nor things present, nor things to come,

Nor height, nor depth, nor any other creature, shall be able to separate us from the love of God, which is in Christ Jesus our Lord.

ROMANS 8:38–39

WHEN
we've
BEEN
THERE

TRULY MY SOUL waiteth upon God: from him cometh my salvation.

HE ONLY IS my rock and my salvation; he is my defence; I shall not be greatly moved.

PSALM 62:1–2

THE GRASS WITHERETH, the flower fadeth: but the word of our God shall stand for ever.

ISAIAH 40:8

TEN
Thousand
YEARS

BRIGHT
shining

THE LORD IS my light and my salvation; whom shall I fear? the Lord is the strength of my life; of whom shall I be afraid?

PSALM 27:1

*A*RISE, SHINE; for thy light
is come, and the glory of the Lord is risen
upon thee.

ISAIAH 60:1

AS THE
sun

WE'VE NO LESS *days*

I AM CRUCIFIED with Christ: nevertheless I live; yet not I, but Christ liveth in me: and the life which I now live in the flesh I live by the faith of the Son of God, who loved me, and gave himself for me.

GALATIANS 2:20

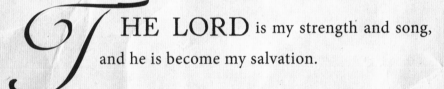

THE LORD is my strength and song, and he is become my salvation.

EXODUS 15:2

TO *sing*

I WILL PRAISE THEE,

O Lord, with my whole heart; I will
shew forth all thy marvellous works.

PSALM 9:1

THAN *when*

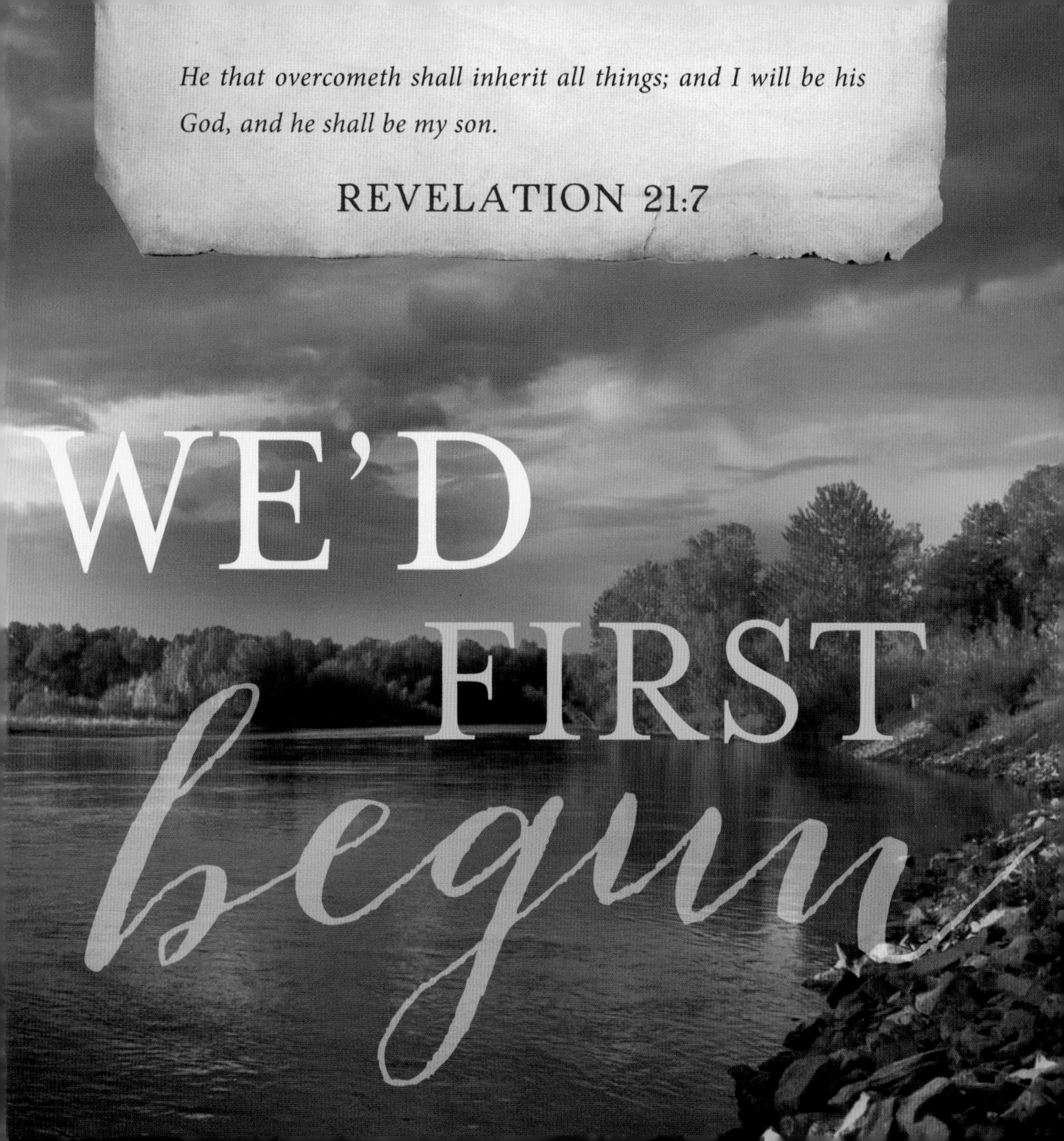

He that overcometh shall inherit all things; and I will be his God, and he shall be my son.

REVELATION 21:7

WE'D FIRST *begun*

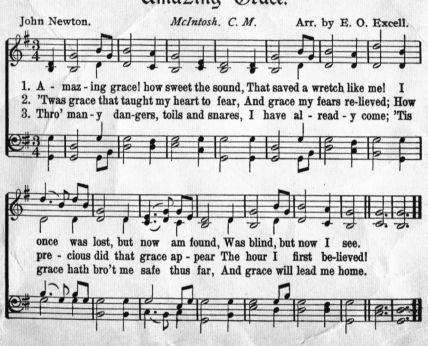

Amazing Grace.

John Newton. McIntosh. C. M. Arr. by E. O. Excell.

1. A - maz - ing grace! how sweet the sound, That saved a wretch like me! I
2. 'Twas grace that taught my heart to fear, And grace my fears re-lieved; How
3. Thro' man - y dan-gers, toils and snares, I have al - read - y come; 'Tis

once was lost, but now am found, Was blind, but now I see.
pre - cious did that grace ap - pear The hour I first be-lieved!
grace hath bro't me safe thus far, And grace will lead me home.

4. The Lord has promised good to me,
   His word my hope secures;
   He will my shield and portion be
   As long as life endures.

5. Yes, when this flesh and heart shall fail,
   And mortal life shall cease;
   I shall possess, within the veil,
   A life of joy and peace.

6. The earth shall soon dissolve like snow
   The sun forbear to shine;
   But God, who called me here below,
   Will be forever mine.

7. When we've been there ten thousand years,
   Bright shining as the sun,
   We've no less days to sing God's praise
   Than when we'd first begun.

AMEN.

Music found at http://freehymnal.com/png/amazinggrace.png; accessed April 4, 2014.

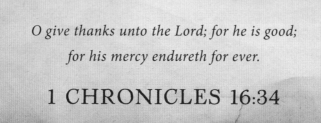

O give thanks unto the Lord; for he is good;

for his mercy endureth for ever.

1 CHRONICLES 16:34

AMEN.

ANGELA BAXTER is an award-winning
graphic designer who has worked in the publishing
industry for eight years. She has a love for all hymns, and
Amazing Grace holds a special place in her heart. She lives
in Utah with her husband, Robert.